Preschool Special Needs

Classroom 911

A Manual for New Teachers

Jennifer Chop

Thank you for purchasing my book. I'd love it if you'd write a review!

For David, Lydia, and Bizzy. You've made my life whole and meaningful.

This book is also dedicated to my colleagues at the Robert R Shearer Preschool in Pleasant Hill, California and the hundreds of students who passed through my class.

Special Thanks

Monique Chapman Homesley and Mary Tsiftsi—Because when I retired, you whispered in my ear something to the effect that wouldn't it be great to have a how-to-do book. The seed was planted and here it is.

Elizabeth Hemphill—Without your editing, the first draft would not have made logical sense. And thank you for taking photographs of the classrooms.

Leslie and Dan Wormhoudt—How can I thank you for taking time to read this manual. The suggestions were followed to the letter. You are such a positive force!

David Hemphill—You are my dearest, sweetest companion who worked too many nights making this book look like a book.

Tina Lopez—Thank you for helping me with the list of iPad Apps that are practical and useful.

Glenda Lightfoot and Lori Williams—Your positive feedback about the value of this manual encouraged me to finish it. Thank you for allowing pictures to be taken of your classrooms.

Kathy Egan—Your constructive brainstorming in the beginning of this project about including the area of speech and language made so much sense. Thank you!

Jody Underhill—Thank you for convincing me that this book should be written to help others.

TABLE OF CONTENTS

INTRODUCTION

You are enough
You have influence
You are a genius
You have a contribution to make
You have a gift that others need
Your actions define your impact
You are the change
You matter
-Angela Maiers

Teaching preschool children with special needs is not for the faint of heart. It's a profession that requires an agile mind and a compassionate heart. As someone who has chosen this field, you are undoubtedly an idealistic person who loves working with young children.

While the job is not easy, there are numerous tricks and tips—contained in this book—which you can learn that will help the day-to-day classroom experience run smoothly. For over thirty years, I taught children with a variety of mild to moderate special needs, including severe oral language disorders, autism, hearing impairment, and cognitive impairment.

That experience helped me to discover time-tested, effective classroom strategies. Over the years I had the privilege of mentoring countless new teachers, and I helped them use these strategies in the classroom.

Do you wish you knew…

- *What to do before the first day of teaching?*
- *How to organize the day?*
- *What to do during Circle Time?*
- *How to integrate movement?*
- *How to teach language skills through play?*
- *How to provide a calm environment?*

Then this book is for you! It's really more of a "manual," because it provides a simple framework for setting up and running your classroom. My hope is that it will reduce the understandable anxieties you might have about starting up your own classroom for the first time.

Don't be afraid to be unconventional—think outside the box when you're teaching. In a mild to moderate classroom the abilities of the children can vary widely.

There will be some children with language delays, others with fine motor and gross motor needs, and still others with cognitive delays. You may have three-year-olds who have no language, and others who are at the one word-stage.

There may be some children with behavior problems who, because of sensory motor integration problems, appear to have aggression issues. You will learn about a wide range of children, and you'll be constantly amazed at the complexity of the human brain!

In teaching young children, you have to be flexible. They bring their own unique energy to the classroom, resulting in ever-changing dynamics. Get to know your new students so that you can adjust your teaching accordingly. Find out what motivates each child. This will require you to observe, assess, and act. You already have these skills, but they will become stronger over time as you gain experience.

Why did you get into teaching? It was probably not in order to worry about setting up and managing a classroom. The tips in this manual will help you become the teacher you want to be, without dwelling on the stress of setting up your classroom. This book lets you focus on what you actually want to do—TEACH!

A good head and a good heart are always a formidable combination.
-Nelson Mandela

CHAPTER ONE

BEFORE YOUR FIRST DAY

The beginning of the school year requires preparation. The good news is that you only need to do it once. Here are five steps to help you prepare for the school year:

1. ***Review Each Student's Individual Education Plan (IEP)***

2. ***Introduce Yourself to Parents***

3. ***Set Up Your Room, Including Center Areas***

4. ***Prepare Circle Time Activities***

5. ***Establish the Rules***

1. Review Each Student's Individual Education Plan (IEP)

You will discover information about each of your students when you read their IEPs, including their family and medical history, development history, and necessary additional services. Here are some things to highlight while reviewing student IEPs:

Food Allergies

By finding out about food allergies (such as peanuts, tree nuts, wheat, dairy, or eggs) emergencies can be avoided. Set up a chart with names and allergies of all students. Keep it posted in the classroom at all times. Omit these items from cooking and art projects to prevent medical emergencies.

If medical emergencies are not promptly treated, children with allergies may exhibit skin, respiratory, digestive, or cardiovascular difficulties. You will then need to act quickly and have the office staff contact parents and emergency services. If a student has been prescribed an epinephrine (adrenalin) auto injector or epipen (which should be with the child at all times) you will have to learn to use it, in addition to calling 911.

Toilet-Training Status

Is the child toilet trained? Has the child exhibited signs that s/he is ready for potty training? If not, you will need a supply of diapers and wipes. Work with the parents to develop a schedule to teach the child when to use the toilet.

Because most children are potty-trained between 18-24 months, parents may not know how or why their 3-, 4-, or 5-year-old child is not yet potty-trained. The following are some signs that a child is ready for potty training. The child can:

- *Follow simple instructions*
- *Understand words about the toileting process*
- *Control the muscles responsible for elimination*
- *Verbally express the need to use the toilet*
- *Keep a diaper dry for 2 hours or more*

- *Get to the toilet, sit on it, and then get off the toilet*
- *Pull down diapers, disposable training pants, or underpants*
- *Show an interest in using the toilet or in wearing underpants*

Other Services that May be Needed

Speech therapy, occupational therapy, physical therapy, behaviorist, vision specialist, adaptive P.E. teacher, etc.

Since you are the Case Manager, it is up to you to contact all the specialists involved in your student's team to ensure that proper services are provided. Establish a relationship so that you and the specialists are able to work together as a team to help the student.

Areas that Need Specific Remediation

Vocabulary, understanding questions, making requests, or self-help skills.

Look at the student's vocabulary and language needs, preschool academic needs, occupational therapy and physical therapy needs, visual needs, adaptive P.E. needs, and self-help needs.

Make a separate folder for each child with his/her IEP. This will be the teacher copy of the IEP, separate from the Cumulative (Cum) folder that is centrally maintained.

Always document what you have done related to each child, with the dates and names of the contacts, and summary of any communication with parents, advocates, or specialists, Keep all such information in the student's folder. It is important to document all information like this in the event of future questions, including parent grievances, legal proceedings, etc. You never know when you will need this sort of information in the future.

2. Introduce Yourself to Parents

Try to meet the parents and children the day before school begins so that the children have a chance to become familiar with their new classroom and you have a chance to meet face-to-face with the parents. If possible, schedule a block of time to “meet and greet ” the day before school starts.

Introduction Letter to Parents

Write a parent letter to introduce yourself and your assistant(s). Be sure to detail what the child should bring to school daily (diapers/pullups, baby wipes, snack or lunch, change of clothing), classroom schedule, and the telephone number or email address where parents can reach you. Send this home on the first day of school.

Here is a sample letter:

9/2/15

Dear Family,

Welcome to Room 14! My name is XXXXX XXXXX and I will be your child's teacher. My assistants are Jackie Brown and Florinda Cortex.

Please supply a backpack for your child so that s/he can bring

- *Snack or lunch, depending on your child's schedule*
- *A set of extra clothing*
- *Diapers and wipes if your child is not yet potty-trained*

Family notes and artwork will be also sent home daily.

Early bird children come to school from 8:45 -11:45 AM.

Late bird children come to school from 11:00 AM-2:00 PM.

The best time to reach me by phone is before school at 8:00 AM or after school at 2:15 PM. You can reach me by calling the school number:

<u>123-456-7890.</u>

Or, email me at:

emailaddress@domain.com

Welcome again!

XXXXX

Basic Forms of Communication with Parents

There are four basic ways to communicate with parents: phone, email, communication notebook, and daily letter.

Phone

Make sure you take notes of your phone conversations with parents and write up a summary. Send a copy of your notes to parents and have them sign and return the copy acknowledging the information discussed. A paper trail is important if legal issues arise later.

Email

Keep copies of all correspondence in a separate file for each child (as noted above). Have parents indicate that they have read your note by responding via email. Print these out and put them in the child's file.

Communication Notebook

Each child should have a notebook that goes from school to home and back again. This is a wonderful way for parents to include photos of an event the child has experienced that can be shared with the class at Circle Time in order to elicit language.

Be sure to have parents write newsy things about their child, such as places they went on the weekend, or a grandparent's visit. This helps with the connection between school and home.

During Circle Time or a quiet time with the student, you can ask questions about the events: "Where did you go with Mommy and

Daddy yesterday?" "Did you go on a long car ride? What did you see?" By eliciting descriptions of events or objects, you will help children to remember and verbalize activities.

Daily Letter

Another way to communicate with parents is through a daily letter. If you have time to write a daily letter, you can use it to report on activities performed during the school day, books read, art projects, the "star" of the week, or other events. If you send home the students' daily art projects, then the daily letter will explain what the art project is about. Some teachers write a weekly letter.

All these forms of communication should be reciprocal. Often parents are too busy with work or other events in their lives to acknowledge that the communication notebook or daily letter has been read, to give any kind of feedback, or to report about events with their child. Nonetheless, try and establish some kind of system so you know that parents have read your notes sent home, such as signing their name next to the note and returning it to you.

In summary, do what you can! Put your system in place to begin with. Then improve on it as each semester goes by.

3. Set Up Your Room, Including Center Areas

Basic Equipment

The following list contains some basic equipment and supplies you will need for your classroom:

- CD player or MP3 player and speakers for singing and motor activities.

- Nametags made out of theme-related shapes and images, laminated, with magnetic strips on back (if using magnetic board) or Velcro (if using felt board).

- Clearly visible names on cubbies, and/or coat hooks. Add students' pictures to the cubbies or coat hooks to aid in identification and reinforce written names.

- White magnetic board, felt board, or corkboard for placing Circle Time items, such as students' names, themes, shapes, numbers, jobs, daily schedule, or weather chart.

- Books to be read during Circle Time.

- Blocks, trains, cars, animals, playdough, people, Legos, puzzles, pretend food (made by collecting empty food boxes from parents and stuffing with styrofoam).

- Crayons, paper, washable paint.

- Photographs of students to use in name game activities and art projects throughout the year.

Classroom Design and Layout

The design of your classroom will be influenced by the amount of space you have. Classroom layout can encourage either positive or negative behaviors.

Certain areas of the classroom should flow openly, but other areas should well defined and self-contained. Areas that are very open are tempting for kids to run through or drive their cars and trucks through, using the spaces as roadways to speed through the class. Instead, divide up the classroom by using furniture for boundaries and “dead ends” to prevent children from zooming around the room.

Make sure that noisy and quiet areas are at opposite ends of the room. The area where students play with vehicles and build with blocks will be noisy, and it will be a wonderful place to encourage socialization and language skills. However, you will also need quiet areas for kids who like books or puzzles, or are overwhelmed by the noisier areas of the classroom.

Cubby areas, boxes, or baskets clearly labeled with each child’s name and their picture will help teach routines. This will provide a regular place to place belongings and artwork.

Center Areas

Set up various activity centers in your classroom for free play. There should be an art area, a toy area, a book area, etc. See two possible room layouts below, and Chapter 3 (The Importance of Play and Center Activities), for more information on center materials.

Here are two different examples of possible classroom layouts:

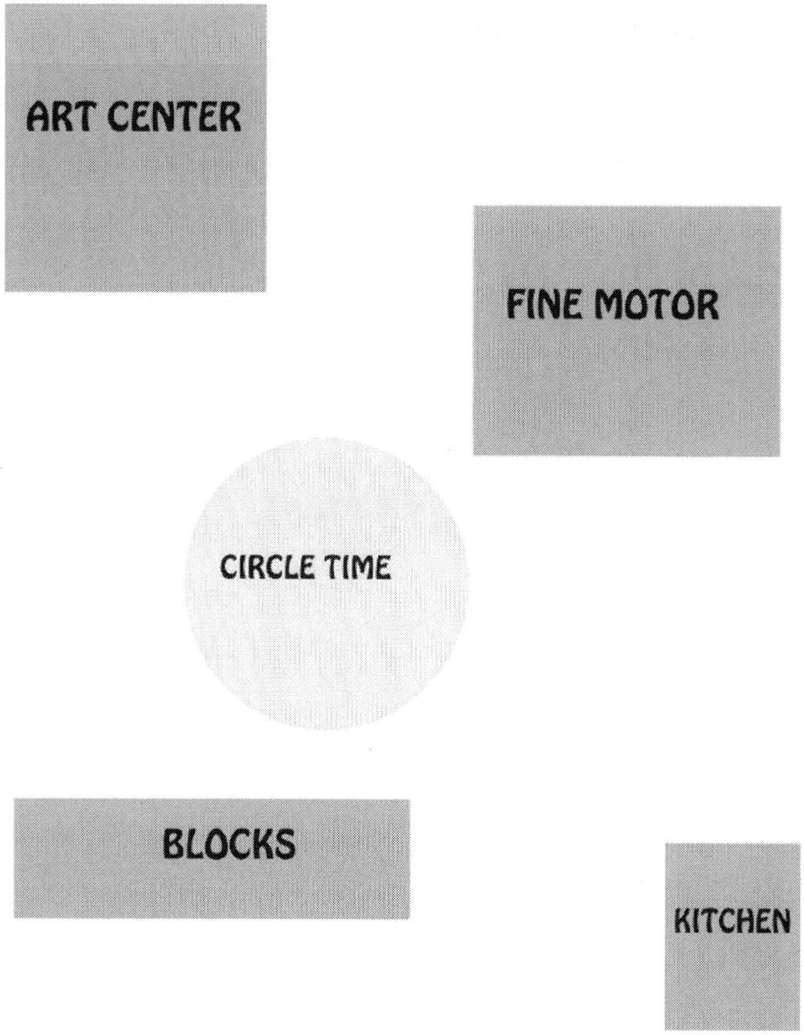

ART CENTER

FINE MOTOR

CIRCLE TIME

BLOCKS

KITCHEN

COAT RACKS

CUBBIES

CIRCLE TIME

BLOCKS

DOOR

PLAY AREA

KITCHEN
AND
DRESS-UP

LIBRARY

COMPUTER
CENTER

TOILET

4. Prepare Circle Time Activities

Decide where and how you will hold Circle Time. It is the central component in the preschool teaching day.

Do you want your students to be sitting on the floor or on chairs? Will you be providing floor mats?

Based on my experience of teaching hundreds of preschool kids, I prefer chairs for two reasons. First, chairs provide stability for kids who have balance problems. Second, chairs offer a physical means to help kids feel a sense of body space.

But observe how your own students react. Maybe they prefer to sit on the floor (for example, on laminated stars or floor cushions). Be open and flexible. Make changes when needed.

After you decide on how the students are going to sit, then pick your Circle Time themes and activities for the first few weeks. The section on Circle Time in Chapter 2 has some suggestions.

5. Establish the Rules

Be sure to establish guidelines for expected behavior during the first several weeks.

- *Keep the rules simple*

- *Review the classroom rules daily*

Visual aids are great for reinforcing rules. Here is a wonderful idea from Lola Ragan, a preschool special educator taken from the following URL:

http://preschoolwondersblog.blogspot.com/

The classroom rules above were embellished with Amazing Mr. Potato Head Parts! Try something like this in your own class, or use other visuals for reinforcement.

Make your own rules and visuals!

- *Use Boardmaker, photographs, or drawings depicting an action or rule.*
- *Be sure to label the rule.*
- *Paste the image and text onto a tongue depressor or similar object.*
- *Hold up the rule during circle time if students are unruly. This will remind children to control their behavior.*

Raise Your Hand

Think about investing in a visual timer or a big red stop sign to signal, or ring a bell when it's time to end certain activities.

Remember to review rules daily during Circle Time for the first several weeks. This reinforces that the rules are important. Repetition helps students internalize the rules.

CHAPTER TWO

HOW TO ORGANIZE YOUR DAY

1. Sample Schedule for a Class Day

Here is a sample of a class schedule for two groups of students overlapping in the mid morning:

First Group Arrives

8:45-9:00 am	Arrival and outside play
9:00-9:30	Circle time
9:30-10:15	Center activities/free playtime
10:15-10:30	Cleanup and potty
10:30-10:50	Snack time
10:50-11:15	Outside recess

Second Group Arrives

11:15-11:45	Large Circle Activities (play Duck, Duck, Goose, musical chairs, group music, etc.)
11:45	First Group goes home
11:45-12:15 pm	Circle time for the Second Group
12:15-12:45	Lunchtime
1245-1:20	Center Activities
1:20-1:45	Second Circle time
1:45-2:00	Closing and departure

The chapters that follow will go into more detail on the activities listed in the preceding schedule, which is divided into Circle Time, Music, Center Time, and Free Playtime.

2. Daily/Weekly Preparation

Preparing the following things ahead of time will make the day run smoothly!

Before Class

- Set up chairs for Circle Time before class begins.

- Prepare laminated nametags in theme-related shapes or pictures, backed by Velcro or divided into magnets. The theme might be the week's story or something related to seasons or holidays.

- Provide a big gym ball for circle activities to engage students in motor movements at the same time.

- Prepare a book and an art project to go along with the book.

After the students arrive

- Students put their backpacks in a designated space. They have 5 to 10 minutes of play in the yard.

- When it is time for class, they pick up their backpacks and carry them into class.

- They find their cubbies or coat hooks with their names and pictures. You can help with identification by attaching a photo of each child beside his/her name.

3. Circle Time

Try to be a rainbow in someone's cloud.
-Maya Angelou

Circle Time is the primary teaching time in the classroom. It is also the first thing that happens in the school day, and you can set the tone for the rest of the day by creating a welcoming atmosphere for children when they arrive.

Neither you nor your assistants will know what kind of morning children have had before school begins, but you can affect the tone of the rest of their day through your initial interactions with them. Use Circle Time to create a sense of togetherness and cooperation.

Set the Atmosphere

All children should feel that school is a safe place. They should also want to come to school because it is fun! Because your students are so young, it may be hard for them to separate from their families. So the classroom needs to become an extended family for them. Even if you've had a tough morning, put that aside and welcome students into the classroom with a smile.

When the day begins positively, children will usually respond in the same way. Action songs teach motor skills and responses to music that produce the powerful learning responses from children. Children also respond to certainty and constancy. The beginning of the day at school should be *fun*.

Make a Circle

You could use chalk to draw a large circle so the children know the boundaries to follow if they are having trouble making a circle. Everybody gets up to form a circle and sings a transition song, such as, "Make a Circle" (to the tune of "Are You Sleeping?"). Children sit on chairs, cushions, carpet squares, laminated stars, or some other designated individual space arranged around the circle. Here are the words to "Make a Circle":

"Make a Circle"
Make a circle, make a circle,
Make it round, make it round.
Joining hands together, joining hands together
Now stand still, now stand still.
(or "Now sit down," or whatever else suits the occasion)

Do a Roll Call

This is a great time to teach the students to recognize their names, the first letter of their names, or the names of other students. There is a detailed procedure for Roll Call described at the end of this chapter.

Begin Circle Time with the Same "Hello" Song Every Day

The best way for children to learn is through repetition. By using the same routine every day, you will teach consistency and predictability. Performing physical movements to songs also teaches children to fill in words and complete actions, which reinforces language learning.

Get Them Moving!

Start the day with songs that involve physical actions. Children need to—and like to—move around. Many children may not yet have well-developed verbal language skills, but they will still be able to learn through physical movement. So you can sing movement songs that everyone moves to in order to teach action words. Here are some examples:

- *"Ring-Around-the Rosie":* Kids love falling down
- *"Motorboat, Motorboat":* You can change the vehicle, the sounds, and the movements
- *"Row, Row, Row, Your Boat":* Have the students work in pairs and act out rowing with each other
- "We Fall Down" (Volume 3, Track 6, from Super Simple Learning, available online at http://supersimplelearning.com/songs/original-series/three/we-all-fall-down/): This song uses a variety of actions and sounds that engage students

Have children use a gym ball or physio ball. The gym ball wakes up their bodies and helps with skills like balance. Your Occupational Therapist might also suggest some deep pressure exercises for certain children, like having them lie face-down while the teacher rolls the gym ball on their backs for deep pressure.

Songs Are Great Teaching Tools

Use music in Circle Time to teach concepts such as colors, animals, numbers, time concepts (e.g. today, yesterday), etc. See the section on Music for more ideas.

Everyone Likes Stories

Use a storybook to create a curriculum. One story can be used to create an entire themed curriculum. You can teach vocabulary, math, science, art, and more with a single story.

Stories are excellent tools to encourage verbal students to predict what might happen next. (See the section on *Mrs. Wishy Washy* for an example of how a story can be used.) Interactive books are great for teaching turn taking. (On an iPad or other tablet students can also take turns "swiping" through the pages).

Switch It Up

If the students have been sitting for a while, then get them moving again. Try a song or a movement chant that involves clapping hands, stamping feet, and changing the pace of the actions from fast to slow. It is important for students to do both sedentary and physical activities.

A wonderful activity while the students are up is to march around a giant hoop or even a circle drawn on the carpet with chalk. This activity is from the math program "Handwriting without Tears." The circle itself can be a teaching tool. For example, each child can take turns throwing a beanbag into the circle and identifying whether it is "in" or "out. This can be used to teach spatial reasoning, prepositions, or counting objects.

Present the Daily Art Project

You can encourage many skills through structured art projects: fine motor skills, following directions, verbalizing requests for help, creating a narrative, or describing a scene. Write the children's descriptions of their pictures on the back. This will help the families to know what the picture is about when it goes home with the child. They can then discuss the picture at home. Such discussions emphasize the link between school and home and further reinforce language development.

Use a Calendar

Using a monthly or weekly calendar at Circle time has endless teaching possibilities. You can teach number sequence, number identification, days of the week, months of the year, temporal concepts like "before," "after," "today," "yesterday," "tomorrow," and birthdates.

However, after many years of attempting to use a calendar, I found that a traditional calendar was too abstract and advanced for many three-year old special needs children. So I stopped using a formal calendar and instead took pictures of activities that had happened "yesterday" and projects that were going to happen "today." In this way I was still able to teach temporal concepts, sequences, and many of the other concepts touched on above.

What I ended up doing for my older preschool kids (the four-to-five year olds) was to create a simple weekly contextual calendar, beginning in **January.**

I used a whiteboard with dry erase markers, although a felt or corkboard would work just as well. I used photographs or drawings. In this way, I built from the "bottom up" to develop their understanding of time vocabulary concepts (today, yesterday, tomorrow), time-related tenses, and the days of the week—based upon meaningful contexts they had experienced in their own lives. It worked very well.

The following is an example of such a simple weekly contextual calendar.

Sunday	 Home
Monday	 O.T. Time
Tuesday	 Read Mrs. Wishy Washy
Wednesday	 Paint a pig
Thursday	 Music Time
Friday	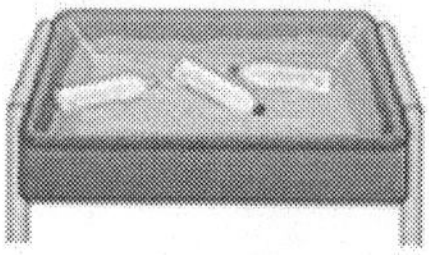 Water Table
Saturday	 Home

Roll Call

This activity teaches children to recognize their own names, their peers' names, and other concepts you may choose.

- Use individual photographs of each student in this daily name game.

- Have a color chart and a clothing chart available so that you or the student can point to the color of the clothing, and so that everyone has a visual reference point.

- Make your own color chart with various colors of construction paper, glued onto cardstock and laminated. If you have access to *Boardmaker* by http://www.mayerjohnson.com, you can produce colors and clothing articles on your computer. (If a student does not match the colors correctly, this tells you that there might be colorblindness, or that s/he does not have concept of matching, or "sameness." Note this in the student's file.)

- Print the students' names on a variety of shapes/colors/theme-related laminated paper and put a strip of magnetic tape on the back, if using a magnetic board at Circle Time.

For example:

In this example, you ask, "Whose name is this?"

On a magnetic board, John takes the apple with his name and places it on or below his picture.

Then ask, "Are you here?" (Students learn how to respond to a question.)

Help John answer, "Yes," or "Yes, I'm here."

Ask John, "What are you wearing today?"

He points or says something about his clothing (color, name of clothing item, etc.)

The whole group sings a song related to the situation. To the tune of "Mary Wore her Red Dress All Day Long," everyone sings:

John is wearing a green shirt,
Green shirt, green shirt
John is wearing a green shirt,
To school today.

In a few weeks, you can assign Roll Call duties to students. The students can do this activity while you facilitate. This activity teaches name recognition, asking questions, responding, and using the form "I'm" or "I am."

In this example, the Roll Call person picks up a nametag, and hopefully has learned to "read" names (or make the association that "John" is an "apple"). He/she asks, "John, are you here?"

John takes his nametag and responds, "Yes, I'm here."

The Roll Call person asks, "What are you wearing?" and John responds with his clothing article and color, either verbally or through gestures.

After putting the nametag on the board, John bounces on the big gym ball, with the teacher supporting him, while everyone sings, "John is Wearing a Green Shirt."

Music

Music is just plain fun. Music is also another way for the brain to receive information. Therefore, teaching cognitive, social, language, and motor skills through music is absolutely appropriate and necessary for preschool children.

Make sure you have a CD player, MP3 player, or tablet. The audio material that you use should include books on tape, simple songs (nursery rhymes, etc.), dancing songs, and even handwriting songs. You can purchase MP3s of individual songs and put them in a playlist in your MP3 player or tablet, plugged into a separate speaker.

If you can play guitar, ukulele, or another portable instrument, that simply adds to the fun! Include musical instruments in your program, like shakers, tambourines, or drums. The kids will love playing instruments to a variety of music. You can even have a mini-performance, where two or three kids choose instruments and perform for the rest of the class. Dress them up with hats!

Below are suggestions for songs to get the school year going. Do a quick Internet search to find the lyrics or music videos for these songs.

- "Eensy-Weensy Spider"
- "Old MacDonald"
- "The ABC Song"
- "Open, Shut Them"
- "Five Green and Speckled Frogs"
- "Five Little Monkeys Jumping on the Bed"
- "Twinkle, Twinkle Little Star"
- "If You're Happy and You Know It"
- "Hokey Pokey"
- "Row, Row, Row Your Boat"

Feel free to ad lib on songs. For example, in "Row, Row, Row Your Boat," ask, "Where else can we row?" Think of all the water places, and what vocabulary you will be introducing.

Music videos are also great for teaching songs. The music videos on the "Super Simple Learning" website are wonderful. They are sung at a slower pace than many commercial children's CDs. The words make sense to young children because of the simple visuals . Motions are also clearly demonstrated. Over time, you will begin to see the students participate in the singing and the actions.

The following are some useful Internet resources that offer music for use with kids:

- Super Simple Learning: http://supersimplelearning.com/
- National Institute of Environmental Health Sciences: http://kids.niehs.nih.gov/games/songs/childrens/index.htm
- Handwriting Without Tears: http://hwtears.com/gss/learning-lounge/music (music available for purchase)
- Talk It and Rock It (formerly Kids Express Train): https:// talkitrockit.com/ (music available for purchase)

4. Sample Theme to Introduce in Circle Time: *Mrs. Wishy Washy*

Incorporating seasonal fall images helps kick start the first several weeks of school. A farm unit is a great way to begin. There are so many books about farm animals, but my favorite is *Mrs. Wishy-Washy* by Joy Cowley.

This is a very simple and repetitive book. It is about a pig, a cow, and a duck that play in the mud. Each one says, "Lovely mud." When Mrs. Wishy Washy finds them, she shrieks and gives each one a bath, with sound effects, and repeats "wishy-washy" over and over.

When she is done washing them and goes back into the house, the animals jump back into the "lovely mud." This website, http://makinglearningfun.com, has wonderful curriculum ideas and templates for this story and numerous other stories.

The following are some ideas for a *Mrs. Wishy-Washy* theme:

Circle Time

- Dress up as Mrs. Wishy-Washy with a bandana and an apron to introduce the story. Have duck, pig, and cow stuffed animals or puppets available to use to act out the story.

- Nametags for Roll Call: cow, pig, duck

- Vocabulary words: cow, pig, duck, mud

- Literacy: Read the story daily. Focus on the letter /p/ since it is very easy to see how it is produced with the exterior of the lips. The letter /p/ is composed of a straight line and a curved line. Practice making /p/ sounds. Tear strips of Kleenex to hold in front of kids' faces. Then try to "pop" the lips to make the Kleenex strips move.

- Math: Tape pictures of a cow, pig, and duck to the floor. Ask the children to jump on 1, 2, or 3 animals to reinforce the concepts of the numbers "1," "2," or "3."

- Music: Learn to sing "Old MacDonald Had a Farm (but substitute "Mrs. Wishy-Washy Had a Farm").

- Art: This photo shows an example of a pig masks made by students working on the "Mrs. Wishy Washy" unit.

Pig masks

With an outline of a cow, use dot markers or slightly blown up balloons dipped in paint to make spots on the cow. A duck can be collaged with feathers.

Center Activities

Art

- For very young children, have cutouts of the animals and have the students fingerpaint or use crayons or markers to make the animals "dirty."

- Fingerpaint with brown paint or chocolate pudding for the background scene and put the three animals in the mud, with the title "Lovely mud."

- At the easel, make a large outline of the animals to be painted (with paints or sponge paint).

Science

- Make mud with dirt and water.

Water

- At the water table, add baby shampoo or bubble bath solution to the water so the students can make bubbles and wash plastic animals.

Apples and other autumnal vegetation make for great themes as well. The following books are great for the beginning of the year.

Apples by Gail Gibbons
The Apple Pie Tree by Zoe Hall
Apples and Pumpkins by Anne F. Rockwell
Nuts to You! by Lois Ehlert

The following activities are also great for the beginning of the year:

- Apple nametags

- Buy an assortment of different colored apples to examine and taste.

- Art: make apple prints by cutting an apple in half and dip it in paint

- Science: Cut open the apple, and look at the seeds. Tell the kids that seeds grow into an apple tree and the blossoms turn into apples on the tree! This is a good sequencing activity.

- Magic (Science): Discover a star in the apple when the apple is cut horizontally

- Math: Count the seeds

- Literacy: Learn the letter A and sounds associated with that letter.

- Bulletin Board: Make or paint a brown trunk and have students make handprints for leaves. Glue student-cut apples onto tree.

These ideas can all be applied to *Mrs. Wishy Washy* and to apple stories, but you can do activities like these with any story! Hopefully, these ideas will spark your own ideas. Look at the details in any story you read, and expand on them for vocabulary and activities.

Remember that repetition is very important. It takes time for information to sink in for the kids. You can plan themes for the rest of the school year, but also observe what your students are interested in, and be flexible!

Themes

Here are some possible themes for the school year:

September: Friendship, school buses, apples, fall, playing with mud

October: Farm, owls, cats, bats, Halloween

November: Transportation, family, Thanksgiving

December: Trains, holiday themes

January: New Year, winter, bears, dinosaurs

February: Shadows, colors, Valentine's Day

March: Wind, kites, St. Patrick's Day, Spring

April: Peter Rabbit, baby animals, gardening

May: Flowers, frogs, Mother's Day

June: Camping, beach, Father's Day

Always remember that the Internet is your friend. Feel free to borrow from ideas that are already out there, and make them your own! Do a web search for whatever theme you want to explore (for example, "apple curriculum for preschool"). There are lots of suggestions out there.

Here are a few websites to help plan your classes. There are more resources in the Appendix:

http://childcareland.com/

www.preschool-plan-it.com

http://preschoolwondersblog.blogspot.com

http://supersimplelearning.com/

www.makinglearningfun.com

http://filefolderheaven.com/preschool-activities

http://more.starfall.com/info/curriculum/pre-k.php

http://readitonceagain.com/

http://preschoolexpress.com/

http://kizclub.com/

https://talkitrockit.com/

CHAPTER THREE

THE IMPORTANCE OF PLAY AND CENTER ACTIVITIES

Play is the work of the child.
-Maria Montessori

1. The Importance of Play

Students learn by exploring. Your room should have different areas for different activities, where students can explore through play. After structured Circle Time, they will need some exploration time. When you dismiss children for free playtime, ask what they want to do and where they want to play.

Play is an essential part of child development and a vital part of the way preschool children learn about life. What does play teach?

- *Risk-taking*
- *Moving through space to find out what is and is not safe*
- *Self-direction*
- *Impulse control*
- *Social interactions*
- *Role-playing*
- *Sharing*
- *Imagination and curiosity*
- *Critical thinking*
- *Communication*

- *Problem-solving*
- *Spontaneity*
- *Empathy*
- *Thinking outside of the box*
- *Turn-taking*
- *Joyfulness*

Observe Your Students

Watch them as if you are at a social gathering to determine how much adult support is needed. Some students will not know how to enter into a play situation. Others will not know what to do with toys except to place them in and out of bins. For both of these sorts of children, you should intervene to provide language structures and model appropriate play.

When you observe your students, ask yourself if they are able to:

- *Learn to cooperate with others?*
- *Figure out how things work?*
- *Build muscle control and strength?*
- *Pick up new ideas?*
- *Use their imagination?*
- *Solve problems?*

If not, you might have to intervene. Here is an example:

- If a child loves cars and trucks, make a ramp and see what s/he does with it.

- If the cars are lined up in a row, take a car and make it go down a ramp. You can verbalize things like, "Go" or "Car go," depending on the language level.

- As children are able to model the word in this playful turn-taking situation, they are also figuring out how a ramp works and will try all kinds of objects. Then, like scientists, they will test their theory of what kinds of things roll.

- Later, you can add more descriptions, such as, "Red car go!" or "Go fast!" Eventually, longer sentence structures can be modeled.

Puzzles and Manipulatives

Puzzles and manipulatives are multi-faceted teaching tools. They can be used to improve language, memory, and social skills, and they can teach problem solving, concepts, eye-hand coordination, and shape identification. For example, figuring out which puzzle piece fits into a particular shape teaches spatial reasoning.

Accomplishing something challenging builds up students' self-confidence and encourages them to take on more challenges. Recalling size, color, and shapes build students' memory skills.

Ask yourself these questions when thinking about which puzzles and manipulatives to use in your classroom:

- *Will the students learn how to problem-solve?*
- *Will the students learn preschool academic concepts?*
- *Will the students develop eye-hand-coordination?*
- *Will the students learn cooperation and sharing if doing puzzles with peers?*
- *Will the students develop cognitive strategies (e.g., matching by shape, color, etc.)?*
- *Will the students learn vocabulary and language skills when interacting with the teacher?*

These are also questions you should ask yourself when you're observing a student playing with puzzles and manipulatives. The questions can help you and other members of the student's IEP team assess the skills of your students in order to address areas that may need specific remediation.

2. Center Activity Area Checklists

I have listed some possibilities for activity centers and a short, accompanying list of basic items for each center area. You will be accumulating more "stuff" as the year goes on, but these items should help you get started in your new classroom.

Art Area

The following are some supplies to consider for the art area:

- Scissors on a tray or holder
- Easels
- Paint cups or juice containers to hold paint
- Paint brushes, foam brushes, roller brushes
- Containers of white glue or glue sticks
- Craft sticks
- Playdough and cookie cutters, rolling pins
- Shaving cream
- Sink
- Sponges
- Crayons, markers
- Newsprint
- Construction paper

My favorite area is the Art Center. Art can be structured, and it can be based on a story read in class. The story's artwork can be used to reinforce the students' language skills by having the students make comments about the picture. What does the picture show? Is it a specific scene from the book? Is there an action word learned from the story?

This is where the special education classroom may differ from the general education classroom. The purpose of structured art is to teach vocabulary from a story in art form. It also practices these skills: following directions, learning sequences, and finally, modeling a sentence or word about the picture or object the students have made.

Comments can be written on the back of the picture and sent home the same day the project is completed so that parents can talk to their child about it. In this way, art projects can be a great way for parents to elicit conversation about what students did at school. Kids should also be encouraged to explore art materials during free playtime.

Art projects can also be simply experimental and sensory: fingerpainting, coloring with crayons or chalk, cutting paper, using playdough, doing watercolors, making collages with paper, playing with beans, sand, or pebbles, making masks, stringing beads for bracelets, etc.

Kitchen Area

- Play stove
- Play sink
- Play refrigerator
- Play food (even something like empty food containers packed with Styrofoam works)
- Plastic cups, plates, utensils
- Pots and pans
- Table and chairs

Book Area

- Comfortable cushions, bean bags, large pillows, child-sized sofa for sitting and reading books
- Bookshelf filled with appropriate books
- Puppets and a puppet stage
- Stuffed animals (for comfort)

Manipulatives Area

- Puzzles
- Matching games
- File games
- Pegs and pegboards

Block Area

- Wooden blocks
- Big cardboard brick blocks
- Smaller blocks of different shapes and colors
- Wooden train tracks and trains
- Vehicles
- Plastic animals (farm, zoo, dinosaurs, etc.)
- Legos

Dress Up Area

- Dress up clothes for both boys and girls
- Baby dollies
- Purses, bags
- Scarves,
- Masks
- Hats

Science Area

- Objects from nature (leaves, pinecones, seashells)
- Magnifying glass
- Color paddles
- Pictures of nature/animals

- Pets/plants
- Rocks
- Different textured materials
- Scale

Sensory Area

Tubs or a sensory table, filled with:

- Water
- Pebbles
- Feathers
- Styrofoam
- Shredded paper
- Basters, Funnels, Pumps, Pitchers, Sponges
- Sand

Cleaning Supplies for the Classroom

- Hand soap for children
- Broom and dustpan
- Sponges
- Towels
- Dish detergent

Things to Think About

- Are the areas clearly defined and labeled?
- Is your room visually pleasing?
- Are the paintbrushes washed daily?
- Do you have a way for storing and labeling your materials?

- Will you remember to vary the puzzles and books?
- Are there enough cleaning supplies for each child to help clean up?

CHAPTER FOUR

MANAGEMENT STRATEGIES FOR A CALM CLASSROOM

The greatest sign of success for a teacher... is to be able to say, "The children are now working as if I did not exist."
-Maria Montessori

You will have a mix of kids, and every mix has different dynamics. Successful classroom management takes experimentation. After thirty years of experimenting with different classroom management techniques, I've developed some basic strategies. My hope is that the strategies discussed here will shorten your own learning curve so that you can focus most of your time on teaching creatively instead of managing behaviors.

Teaching preschool children self-control will result in a calm classroom. A calm classroom means calm kids. As children mature, it becomes increasingly important that they have the ability to stay calm in a variety of situations, both inside and outside of the classroom. You can have a great impact on their later life by simply creating a calm learning environment for them during their early education.

1. Transitioning To Different Activities

One of the biggest challenges in teaching preschoolers with special needs is learning how to move them from one activity to another without chaos. Children often become upset when their play is interrupted, and they may have difficulty understanding why they need to do something different.

Special needs preschool classrooms can be organized to run smoothly with well-chosen transition activities or objects. By knowing what each child likes, you can tailor successful transition activities.

Helpful Transition Techniques

Here are some proven transition strategies:

- Consistently sing a transition song such as "School Today Is Over." Try Googling "preschool transition songs" or "preschool transitions," to find many other such songs.

- Some kids like to hold things, so a ball or small physical object will calm them down.

- Assign tasks, such as, "Johnny, pick up the farm animals."

- Create cards with visuals of the next activity, and have students hold them.

- Be careful with the words you use. Certain trigger words can cause tantrums. For example, the words, "Clean up" caused major tantrums in my class one year. Yet when the words were switched to "Pick up time," or when children were asked to "Find all the cars," the number of tantrums was reduced.

Cleanup

Cleanup is one of the most contentious parts of the day! This is because free time is over and the children now have to clean up their toys. Here are some quick cleanup tips:

- Get a visual timer. This is a great visual tool for transition times, class schedules, or whenever you want students to complete a task within a given time. A kitchen timer or the timer on a phone or digital tablet can also work. I had an excellent, eight-inch square visual timer with a red display that disappeared as time lapsed. I acquired it from Discount School Supply:

  http://www.discountschoolsupply.com/Product/ProductDetail.aspx?product=27993

- Give a two-minute warning before the timer beeps. When the timer rings, have a student ring a bell or flash the lights.

- Label individual bins and shelves with pictures of toys, so students will know where to replace them.

- Use sign language or flash a picture of students cleaning up toys. This helps students who don't have much receptive language to understand what is being asked of them.

- If needed, assign different children to pick up animals, cars, blocks, or objects by color.

- Reward with stamp or stickers initially, if necessary.

2. Behavior Management Troubleshooting Tips

Keep Their Hands Full

Some kids just need the physical sensation and comfort of holding an object. Balls, fidgets (small toys or gadgets that help with focus, like Tangle, koosh balls, stretchy animals, plastic nuts and bolts, flashing and squishy toys), or other sensory objects can be soothing for these children.

Everyone Likes to be Rewarded

Positive rewards are powerful. Kids love rewards like stickers or stamps; these are tangible positive reinforcements. When students transition well, provide them with some kind of physical reward. Though physical rewards won't always be necessary, they help to jumpstart behavior shifts.

If children refuse a stamp or sticker, it might be that they have sensory issues and do not want anything placed on their skin. In such cases, just put the sticker on a piece of paper and send it home with them. This also shows parents that their students are progressing, and it encourages parents to praise their children at home for learning in the classroom.

Encourage Learning through Focused, Specific Verbal Praise

Recent research shows that specific, focused praise statements such as, "You really are trying," or, "Wow! You put a lot of red on that picture!" help build self-confidence and a sense of responsibility. This is opposed to generalized, unfocused statements like, "Good job." The latter statement does not encourage progress; it only indicates completion.

In the "Good job" scenario, the child has accomplished all s/he needs to do, and has no reason to do anything more. On the other hand, commenting about something that the child is *doing* (not what that child has *done*) is a way of teaching the child that s/he is succeeding in the process of work.

In other words, be specific in your praise. Focus on processes that students are performing. Don't just pass out empty praise that it not tied to specific performances. In addition, try to encourage further performance. Try not to imply that no further development is needed.

Teaching Self-Control Results in a Calm Classroom

It is hard for children to learn when their bodies are not quiet. When they are busy looking at other things or touching peers, children can't pay attention to the teacher. Distribute fidgets during group Circle Time to help kids stay calm. Hold up your visual classroom rules (like images of hand-raising, listening ears, etc.) to help focus attention and reinforce self-control.

Do Yoga

There are numerous "Yoga for Kids" DVDs. Yoga can be especially useful for teaching deep breathing. Deep breathing can use up excess energy in a fun and educational way. Breathing techniques can also be helpful for children when they are angry.

What's Going on Outside of School?

When a child is acting out of sorts, find out if something out of the ordinary happened outside of school. For example, was there a stressful trip to the dentist or the doctor? Did the child have to go to the emergency room because s/he poked her/his eardrum with a Q-tip? Were there other family issues that it would help you to know about?

Use Sensory Objects

If you have access to an occupational therapist, he or she might have suggestions, such as using a weighted vest or animal, sitting on wedges or barely-inflated beach balls, or using certain fidgets. Try to have a supply of fidgets for the whole class during Circle Time. Then be sure and collect them at the end of Circle Time.

Too Much Sensory Information!

For some kids, what appears to be inappropriate behavior may actually be their response to sensory overload. The flickering of fluorescent lights, the noise level in the environment, or even the amount of visual displays in the classroom (such as hanging objects) can contribute to a child who seems "unsettled."

Even tags or labels in clothing rubbing against the child's skin might be the cause of agitation for a child. Cut off the labels. Turn down the lights, if need be.

Use a Timer

As mentioned before, timers are powerful! When it is time for an activity to end, the timer rings. It is the timer that says, "The activity is over," and not you, the teacher. The timer takes the blame away from the adult. "Did you hear that? The timer went 'ding.' Time to clean up." Timers can serve as reinforcements for children who may otherwise "space out."

As an example, children can be asked to perform assigned activities, and then as a reward be allowed to play freely for a specified number of minutes (which you first demonstrate on a timer!) before beginning another teacher-directed activity. This can be useful throughout the day, including helping children to transition among different activities, or to clean up at the end of the day.

Turn taking and sharing are also important skills that children need to learn. When a spat over a toy occurs, the timer can also be the answer to the dispute. You set a specified number of minutes for one child to play with the toy. Then when the alarm rings, it's time for the other child's turn. Make sure the children understand the rule first, of course. Parents can be encouraged to use a timer as well for common problem issues like bedtime, getting dressed, etc.

Remove the Child from the Group as a Last Resort

Disruptive students can be distracting to other students, and sometimes they need a quick break from the group. Have your assistant take the child away from the group to do some kind of solo activity. Here are some simple suggested activities to give an individual child a "breather":

- *Go for a walk*
- *Drink some water*
- *Read a book*

- *Bounce on a large physio ball or trampoline*
- *Go on a swing*

After you've tried your hardest and exhausted all the ways you can think of to calm a child who is angry, and if safety in the classroom is becoming an issue, it might be necessary to have a behaviorist help develop a behavior plan for the child.

Prior to this you should document what you have done, and the situations in which problems have occurred. Use of a simple annotated chart, such as the one provided in Section 3 below, can be useful for documenting student behaviors.

In summary, keep the following points in mind for smooth classroom management:

- *Be sure to develop and follow routines and regular schedules*
- *Decide on a daily reward system*
- *Have a set of fidgets for circle time (if necessary)*
- *Ask an occupational therapist for equipment (weighted vest, wedge, etc.)*
- *Distract the child who is having difficulty in a group situation*
- *Check for sensory overloads*

- *Use a timer to end projects or to help students share a toy equally*

- *Use pictures or drawings of the next activity to help with transitions*

- *Remove the disruptive child from an activity as a last resort*

3. An Example of an Annotated Chart for Behaviors

STUDENT BEHAVIOR NOTES

STUDENT'S NAME: *Xenia*

DATE	OBSERVED BEHAVIOR	ACTION TAKEN
5/1/2014	*Touched peer during Circle Time 3 time. Seems to only happen when Yuri is sitting next to him.*	*Moved Xenia to another spot during Circle Time, away from Yuri.*

Be kind whenever possible. It is always possible.
-Dalai Lama

CHAPTER FIVE

HOW DO YOUR STUDENTS COMMUNICATE?

Because I was trained in speech and language pathology, I was fortunate to be able to teach for 30 years in preschool classes where the students' primary disabilities were speech and language disorders. Your class will probably be composed of students with mixed abilities, but language is emphasized in this section because ***preschool education is based on oral language.***

Take every opportunity to elicit language from your students. Since oral language is a primary component of preschool education, you need a basic understanding of what affects your students' language abilities.

1. Issues that Affect Speech and Language Development

Why do we learn language? The end goal is communication. Words are not simply sounds we make and hear; they are also a means of understanding. Language is about transmitting and receiving signals. It helps us make sense of the world around us, and of one another.

There are a variety of reasons why speech and language development may be delayed in certain students. If students are not speaking or do not seem to understand, they might need additional speech services.

As the primary teacher for your students, you are their case manager. It is therefore up to you to make referrals for issues that may have been overlooked in the initial assessment and placement process.

To assess what might be happening with a particular student's language development, here are some questions to ask about their speech and language skills:

- *Is the student's hearing adequate to hear speech?*
- *Does the student have recurring ear infections or allergies?*
- *Does the student understand what is said?*
- *Does the student use words to communicate?*
- *Does the student have anatomical deviations that affect speech production?*
- *Does the student demonstrate memory abilities?*

Infants learn language by hearing words around them. This shapes their speech production because they imitate what they hear. The first two years of an infant's life are especially crucial for developing speech and language. Repeated ear infections will muffle the sounds heard by young children and create an environment of distorted sounds. Undetected hearing loss is another reason for lack of speech and language development.

It is important to distinguish between comprehension and speech. A student may understand language, but may not be physically able to voice understandable speech. Here are some reasons for speech problems:

- *Articulation* (how sounds are made, e.g. lifting the tongue up behind the top teeth to produce "t")
- *Phonological processes* (sound patterns, e.g. consistently substituting "f" for "tr")
- *Anatomical deviations* (disorders caused by allergies, thumb sucking, enlarged tonsils and adenoids, etc.)
- *Motor Speech Disorder* (weak mouth and facial muscles and respiratory system)
- *Childhood apraxia of speech* (the brain has difficulty planning the movement of sound-producing body parts—lips, tongue, jaw).
- *Stuttering*
- *Voice* (excessively hoarse voice, which might be an indicator of nodes on the vocal chords)

These are areas that the speech pathologist, as part of the student's IEP team, can address. If you see these symptoms in a student, but they are not noted in the IEP, then the speech pathologist may not be aware of them. Thus the student may not be getting the appropriate services. Make sure that everyone on the IEP team is on the same page.

2. Language Disorders

Language disorders may look like behavior problems. Children might appear defiant or sullen when they just don't understand what is being said in a given situation! A student may also appear to be cognitively impaired for the same reasons.

The following lists will help you determine if a child has a language disorder. If you observe any of these, you can bring them up with the child's IEP team to determine the proper course of action. (Sensory processing disorders may also look like behavior problems. There is a sensory processing disorder checklist in the Appendix for your reference.)

I've listed symptoms that many children with language disorders exhibit in the mild to moderate preschool classroom. These lists were adapted from the American Speech-Language-Hearing Association's (ASHA) list of Preschool Language Disorders, available online at:

http://www.asha.org/public/speech/disorders/Preschool-Language-Disorders/.

Receptive Language Disorders

Some children have problems with understanding. These are called receptive language disorders. Children who have receptive language disorders may have trouble with the following skills:

- *Understanding gestures*
- *Following directions*
- *Answering questions*
- *Identifying objects and pictures*
- *Taking turns when talking with others*

Expressive Language Disorders

Some children have problems talking. These are called expressive language disorders. They may have trouble with the following skills:

- *Asking questions*
- *Naming objects*
- *Using gestures*
- *Putting words together into sentences*
- *Learning songs and rhymes*
- *Using correct pronouns, like "he" or "they"*
- *Knowing how to start a conversation and keep it going*

Be Sure to Pause When Eliciting Language

Since students are in your classroom most of the time, take every opportunity to elicit language. Many children have problems with both receptive and expressive language.

Sometimes, students may take as long as five to ten seconds to respond to questions because they need time to process the questions asked. They may give an answer to a question you asked earlier instead of the current one.

When you ask questions of students, pause to let them process. They might surprise you with how much they really do understand and how much they can say! Here are some examples for eliciting language:

- After completing an art project, say, “Tell me about the picture.” Write whatever is said, and then expand upon it. (For example, child says, “Pig”. The teacher expands the utterance: “A pig lives on a farm,” or “Pigs like mud.”)

- After a game, ask, “What did you do?” If students need help opening a container at snack or putting on a jacket, then model the word or sentence or teach the sign, “Help me,” and have them repeat it.

- In the morning, emphasize using words or gestures to greet teachers or friends. For example, the child learns to say “Hi,” smiles, gives eye contact, and gives a “High 5.” Remember, the goal is to help students to communicate effectively, and gestures are a part of this.

- When students have difficulty entering a play situation, give them the words they need, such as "Can I play with you?" In this way you are offering the students a communication model that they can learn to use on their own.

There are many more examples throughout the book of different ways to generate language and communication in different classroom activities. Feel free to come up with your own ideas. Be creative and have fun!

CHAPTER SIX

FURTHER TEACHING TIPS

Expect problems and eat them for breakfast.
-Alfred A. Montapert

This chapter contains some additional teaching tips. These simple tips are surprisingly effective.

General Techniques

- When teaching, face children at eye level. They will be more engaged when you are eye-to-eye.
- Interpret what students are trying to say by expanding on their words or what they are looking at.
- For some kids who have delayed processing, wait 5 to 10 seconds for their responses.

Reading

- You can use a single theme or book to demonstrate concepts (action words, colors, animals) throughout a week. Read a target book daily. Themes are excellent teaching tools. Alternate themes throughout the weeks.
- Repeat concepts often throughout the day/week/month for reinforcement.

- Make a surprise box and put a new mystery item in it every day. This ignites curiosity and encourages communication.

- Use a puppet to introduce concepts and to interact with the students.

- Use interactive books (pop-up, iPad, etc.) to engage the students.

- Make simple books and send them home to reinforce concepts at home (colors, shapes, prepositions, school activities, etc.).

- Engage students while reading a book by having a discussion about each page, checking for comprehension, interest, conversation, and listening skills.

- Teach nursery rhymes. After students have learned the rhyme, have them finish a word or phrase to teach prediction.

- Use visual aids while reading a story (for example, story characters). Act out the story. Read the story over several days during the week for reinforcement.

Music

- Use students' names in songs. Change action words and places in songs. This varies the song, and gives students a point of self-reference.

Math

- Count items daily: Number of classmates, shoes, boys, girls, pockets, buttons, etc.

Art

- Do an art project daily: Finger painting, or coloring with crayons and markers.

- Decorate a large appliance box for a cave or castle or rocket ship; paint on an easel; stamp paper with paint using commercial stamps, kitchen objects, or designs cut from potatoes; make collages with their torn up paper; use playdough; make macaroni necklaces; draw with chalk outside.

- Decorate the bulletin board with theme-related pictures. Try to send students' art projects home daily, as they will be current in students' memories, and the students can talk about their pictures at home.

Structure

- Very young children may require a rope or rope with handles to go outside the classroom to another location. You can find these online at Amazon or Lakeshore Learning. Search for "walking rope."

Jobs

Kids love to have jobs, but make sure that you have a job for everyone! I learned this the hard way when I did not assign a job to everyone. "What about me?" children would ask. They felt they weren't treated fairly.

Jobs are a great way to teach turn taking. Some students always want to be first, but by rotating jobs, they'll learn that they can't always be first.

You can assign jobs at the beginning of the week. Each child spends a week doing the same job, and rotates into another job the following week. Your jobs might include weather reporter, animal helper, etc.

List the jobs (with a visual) in a row on a board entitled "What's Your Job?" Place the students' names next to their assigned jobs, and each week move their names over sequentially so that the leader one week moves back down to become the caboose!

Example:

1. *Star of the Week (leader)* – Joey

2. *Roll Call Helper (passes out nametags)* – Anna

3. *Placemat Helper (passes out placemats at snack or lunchtime)* – Gonzalo

4. *Light Helper (flashes light to indicate cleanup time and turns lights off at the end of the day)* – Cristina

5. *Plant Helper (helps water plants)* – Frankie

6. *Caboose (last person in line – makes sure no one strays)* – Paulina

The next week, Joey becomes the Caboose, Anna becomes the Star of the Week, Gonzalo the Roll Call Helper, and so on.

With *Boardmaker* by Mayer-Johnson (http:// mayer-johnson.com) you can make pictures of these jobs or draw your own.

If you don't like how things are, change it! You're not a tree.
-Jim Rohn

A FEW FINAL WORDS

Don't be discouraged! There will be nights of distress and anxiety about what you are doing and whether or not it is working. With experience, you will get the hang of it.

No one would say that teaching special education is a piece of cake, and it is definitely not for the faint of heart. Always remember why you went into this profession—and that personal insight will be your best guide.

The teaching profession and parents need idealistic teachers like you, who have a vision. Think outside the box and be as creative and as "crazy" as you can in your preschool classroom.

Try to model the special education class after the general education class. Don't shortchange your kids in terms of academic skills. All children can learn, given the right circumstances.

But teach them in a fun way, through play. When you incorporate play into your classroom, children will learn in a natural setting—acquiring social skills (sharing, joining in play situations, turn-taking), language skills, and developmental skills.

Thank you for joining the teaching profession. We're lucky to have you!

Every child deserves a champion: an adult who will never give up on them, who understands the power of connection and insists they become the best they can possibly be.

-Rita Pierson

APPENDIX

Workshops and Guides

These resources are not free, but the skills and activities gained can be used for many years to come.

Read it Once Again *(www.readitonceagain)*
Read it Once Again creates comprehensive early child curriculum that improves speech and language skills, builds cognitive, gross motor, fine motor skills, and integrates lessons on daily living and socialization into story units. There are a total of 30 stories; each comes with a CD loaded with activities.

The first level addresses the skills and the second level works on higher levels of foundational skills using the same story. Each level is $50. The units can last a month for preschool children with mild to moderate disabilities. There is a great *Mother Goose* unit and *Preschool Classroom Management Guide.*

"Get Set for School" *by Handwriting without Tears (http://www.hwtears.com/gss)*
"Get Set for School" is a pre-Kindergarten program with Readiness & Writing, Language & Literacy, and Numbers & Math programs that use multisensory approaches to invite children's participation. The materials and activities are both well thought-out.

The original HWT program was designed by an occupational therapist. The best way to learn this program is to attend a workshop. These fun and idea-packed workshops are held around the country. The music CD that accompanies the program is enjoyable and upbeat. The cost for a full day workshop that includes PK readiness, writing, literacy, and math is about $350 if registered thirty days prior to the workshop. You will also receive $225 in free materials.

"Learning Language and Loving It" *by The Hanen Centre (www.hanen.org/Guidebooks---DVDs/Educators/Learning-Language-and-Loving-It.aspx)*

The Hanen Centre is a wonderful organization with many programs that address communication development in children with language delays. "Learning Language and Loving It" is a guide for teachers who are not speech/language pathologists. This is a guide to help children interact and communicate effectively in early childhood settings. The book and DVD combo pack costs $85.

File Folder Heaven *(http://www.filefolderheaven.com/)*

File Folder Heaven provides printable file folder games, adapted books, cookie sheet activities, and clothespin tasks and Autism tasks. Materials can be downloaded with costs varying from $1 up to $75 for packages.

Talk It Rock It *(https://www.talkitrockit.com/product-category/cds/)*

This company makes wonderful music CDs for speech and language development. The songs teach imitation, language, and sounds with great actions to accompany the music. Separate CDs are $39.99 and the complete set of 5 CDs (includes Imitation, Rock-and-Roll with a Language Goal, Drills, Digo y Canto (for Spanish speakers) and Animals Movin' and Groovin' for $99.99.

Free Internet Resources

Super Simple Learning *(www.supersimplelearning.com)*
This is a great music website with lyrics and videos. Kids enjoy them and learn vocabulary and actions by watching the music videos. Their music videos are on YouTube, and can be accessed with a Gmail address. The website now sells completed video sets at $14.99 each, and Halloween and Christmas videos for $12.99.

Childcareland.com *(http://www.childcareland.com/)*
Teacher Shelly Lovett posts curriculum activities like daily art projects and matching games. You can subscribe for a free email newsletter with teaching tips and downloadable printables.

Explore!
Here are some other useful free sites to explore.

www.preschool-plan-it.com

http://preschoolwondersblog.blogspot.com

www.makinglearningfun.com

http://www.filefolderheaven.com/preschool-activities

http://more.starfall.com/info/curriculum/pre-k.php

http://www.readitonceagain.com/

http://preschoolexpress.com/

http://kizclub.com/

https://www.talkitrockit.com/

Useful DVDs

YogaKids, Vol. 3: Silly to Calm
by Marsha Wenig, directed by Ted Landon
Filled with yoga activities to help kids focus, follow directions. The DVD features a video of the animals that the yoga poses are named after.

Model Me Kids
Available through http://www.modelmekids.com/, these DVDs show situations modeled by peers in a variety of social settings.

Watch Me Learn
Designed for children with autism spectrum disorder, these DVDs available at http://www.watchmelearn.com/ teach skills through video repetition.

Sensory Processing Disorders

The sensory processing disorder is still in the process of becoming accepted and treated. The following website is an excellent resource for questions about particular signs of sensory processing dysfunctions:

http://www.sensory-processing-disorder.com/child-developmental-checklist.html

Use this checklist as a way of observing students when "you can't put your finger on" what's going on with a child aside from cognitive or language delays:

Ever Wonder Why Your Child Does the Things S/He Does? (from the preceding website)

- Do you wonder why they are excessive risk takers—jumping and crashing into anything they can?
- Why they can't do puzzles—write- well—or find the coordination for riding a bike or hitting a ball?
- Why they cry or cover their ears with every loud sound – even vacuums, toilets or hairdryers?
- Why they don't like to touched or can't be touched enough?
- Why they will only eat macaroni and cheese and pizza?
- Why they will only wear certain clothes or need you to cut the tags out of their shirts?

- Ever wonder why you can't seem to calm them down or get them to sleep?

- Why they won't put their hands in anything messy or use glue, playdough, or play with mud?

- Why they fear playground equipment or being tipped upside down?

- Why crowded stores bother them so much leading to major meltdowns in public places?

Downloadable flyers are available at: http://spdfoundation.net/flyer.html for more information on sensory processing disorders.

iPad Apps

A list of helpful websites for newest apps and reviews:

http://blog.momswithapps.com/apps-for-special-needs/, a compilation of suggested apps for children with special needs.

http://kindertown.com/, contains lists of apps for preschool age children

http://www.appfriday.com/, a website that highlights educational apps on Fridays from new developers. Sometimes they are free if you download before 9:00pm (PST). The apps are not only preschool age.

Useful classroom apps for a variety of levels:
Augmentative and Alternative Communication (AAC)
Sono Flex Lite (free)
See, Touch, Learn

Speech and Language:
Speech with Milo
Hamaguchi Apps for Speech, Language & Auditory Development
Talking Tom 2

Alphabet:
Interactive Alphabet ABC'S by Piikea St.
ABC MAGIC 2 BY PRESCHOOL UNIVERSITY
AlphaTots Alphabet by Spinlight Studio

Art:
iLuv Drawing Animals-Learn how to draw 40 animals
Draw with Hearts-Happy Valentine's Day
iLuv Drawing Dinosaurs

Math:
Monkey Math by Thup.com
Bugs and Buttons by Little Bit Studio
Busy Bee's Brainy Bugs by Busy Bee Studios
Little Patterns Toys by GrasshopperApps.com
Counting Bear by Grasshopper Apps
Eddy's Number Party
Giggle Ghosts: Counting Fun!
Twinkle, Twinkle Little Star

Games: (teaching multiple skills)
Injini: Child Development Game Suite
Zoo Train
Peekaboo Barn
Pepi Bath
Preschool Games-Farm Animals

Fine Motor Skills:
Color Squares
Color Dots
Counting Dots
Wet Dry Try by Handwriting without Tears
Family BoatGame

For Younger Children:

Match It Up
Baby Sign
Articulation Pro
Peekaboo HD
Sound?
Talking Santa
SeeTouchLearn
BitsBoard
Nouns
Starfall

ABOUT THE AUTHOR

Retired after thirty years of teaching a class of preschool children with severe oral language disabilities, Jennifer Chop still thinks fondly of the "good old days" of teaching. She has a B.A. from the University of California, Berkeley in Oriental Languages and an M.A. in Speech and Language Pathology from California State University, Sacramento.

Jennifer lives with her wonderful partner, David Hemphill, of forty-three years. She raised two fantastic daughters, on whom she tested out so many of her theories about child development that they often wondered why their toys went missing. In another life, she might have been a toy inventor.

Jennifer loved studying the ways children learned and figuring out what clicked for them. These challenges and solutions manifested in many "aha" moments. Throughout her career she thrived on dreaming up art projects that were fun and messy, and that taught vocabulary and concepts to her students.

Designing water fountains with her students as a way of teaching science and cognitive strategies, and using wooden blocks and cans was one of Jennifer's favorite projects. Dancing around the room to the "Dance of the Clowns" from the *Nutcracker Suite* as a way of learning the concepts "fast" and "slow" was always an activity that elicited peals of laughter from students, as the music's heart-racing movements climaxed at the end of the piece. Parents of past students visited and commented that even though their children were no longer in her class, they still talked often about Jennifer's Chinese New Year's dragons and parades.

These days Jennifer spends her time painting and playing classical guitar, strengthening her right hemisphere skills, and perfecting the art of making beautiful chocolate truffles with glittery tops. She says it's kind of like preschool art. She's also pursuing her love of learning foreign languages: Latin, Arabic, and Italian. When speaking a foreign language, she claims that life is so much simpler if one uses only infinitives. Jennifer also takes daily walks with her rambunctious dog, Lucy, who needs to wear a compression vest to calm down. Well, at least for now.

Made in United States
Troutdale, OR
12/30/2024